DEACONS
IN THE
LITURGY

DEACONS
IN THE
LITURGY

ORMONDE PLATER

MOREHOUSE PUBLISHING
HARRISBURG, PENNSYLVANIA

Morehouse Publishing
PO Box 1321
Harrisburg, PA 17105

Morehouse Publishing is a division of The Morehouse Group.

Cover design by Trude Brummer

Library of Congress Cataloging-in-Publication Data
Plater, Ormonde.
    Deacons in the liturgy / Ormonde Plater.
        p. cm.
    ISBN: 0-8192-1586-6 (pbk.)
        1. Deacons—Episcopal Church.   2. Deacons—Anglican Church of
Canada.   3. Deacons—Anglican Communion.   4. Episcopal Church—
Liturgy. 5. Anglican Church of Canada—Liturgy. 6. Anglican Commuion—
Liturgy. I. Title.
BX5967.5.P53   1992
264'.03—dc20   91-39363
                                                                      CIP

Printed in the United States of America

Contents

Foreword

One of the happy results of the twentieth century renewal of the church is the recovery of the diaconate as a distinctive and functioning order of the ordained ministry. For the first time in centuries, western Christians are actually experiencing the three-fold ministry that catholic Christians believe to have been established in the church "since the time of the New Testament" (BCP 510).

While this recovery was more rapid than many expected, it was not without its hurdles. Some were persuaded—and some still are—that the establishment of a "permanent" diaconate would inhibit the development of genuine lay ministries, or even supplant them. Fortunately, this has proved not to be true. As deacons have reflected on the unique nature of their ministry, it has become increasingly clear that a significant part of it is enabling the ministry of others.

Of this, Deacon Plater has been an eloquent spokesman. In his writings, lectures, and travels, he has persuasively argued the case, and converted many. It has been my particular pleasure to have known and supported him, to have served with him on the Council of Associated Parishes, and to have been part of the early national conferences on the diaconate.

Now it is time for me to commend this book. As the Introduction points out, it can be used with my book, *The Ceremonies of the Eucharist*. But it is good for deacons to have a book of their own, and this is a particularly fine one. *Deacons in the Liturgy* not only sets forth the basics of diaconal liturgy in a convenient format, but sees it in the context of the whole of diaconal ministry. It is, in fact, just what would be expected from one whose scholarship is sound, and who brings to the liturgy a style and verve that is profoundly engaging. To watch Ormonde Plater bear the gospel book in procession is to know what is meant by the ministry of angels.

Howard E. Galley
St. Vincent of Saragossa 1992

Preface

In 1980, the National Center for the Diaconate (now the North American Association for the Diaconate) asked me to write a liturgical manual for use in the Episcopal Church, published the following year as *The Deacon in the Liturgy*. A decade later, I decided to revise it as *Deacons in the Liturgy*.

The revision makes two major changes. First, the book uses the plural. Where once it spoke of *the deacon* in the liturgy, as if most parishes had only one (if they had any), now it speaks of *deacons*. The plural refers to a modest number, appropriate to the dignity and restrained style of Anglican liturgy. In 1980 a deacon in a parish was a rare sight; now in some dioceses it is common to see two or more. Plurality of service also has precedent in scripture. Jesus sent disciples out by twos to bring the good news and to prepare the Passover meal. In serving by twos, deacons symbolize the number and diversity of all Christian ministries of word, care, and worship.

Second, the book treats seriously the teamwork of deacons and other baptized persons. Deacons work with others to adapt, compose, and lead the prayers of intercession. They wait on table so that the others in the assembly can offer a sacrifice of praise and thanksgiving. Joining with others, they serve the messianic meal and send waiters out of the liturgy to feed absent brothers and sisters. By working together in liturgy, deacons and others symbolize the mission of the church in the world.

Mainly, the book is entirely new, extensively revised, rephrased, and expanded. Wherever possible, it avoids religious jargon and tries to make language about deacons, like their style in liturgy, vigorous, plain, and practical.

Morehouse Publishing agreed to make the book available to a wider public. Howard E. Galley once again read the manuscript with his deep knowledge of the traditions of the church and his awareness of liturgical practices in our age. The revision is designed for use in both the Episcopal Church and the Anglican Church of Canada. Page references point not only to American books, but also to the Canadian *Book of Alternative Services*.

Ormonde Plater
St. Francis of Assisi 1991

Introduction

Among many reforms, the Book of Common Prayer adopted by the Episcopal Church in 1979 restored diversity of ministries as a cardinal principle of worship. The 1549 prayer book assumed as the norm a solemn and corporate form of the eucharist. Thereafter, in the Church of England and her sisters of the Anglican communion, bishops, priests or presbyters, deacons, and other baptized persons performed liturgical roles (when they had them) inconsistent with a serious theology of the body of Christ. Prayer books in England and elsewhere presented a liturgy closely related to the medieval low mass. In the typical Anglican eucharist, the priest recited most of the liturgy while the people listened or read along.

The enhanced use of deacons is a notable aspect of reformed liturgy. In the 1549 prayer book, deacons (vested in "Albes with tunacles") performed traditional functions. Afterward, deacons virtually disappeared. In a period extending from the English prayer book of 1662 through the American prayer book of 1928, deacons assisted in the eucharist, but the only role clearly assigned them was to receive the alms, bring them to the priest, and help in the distribution of communion. In the twentieth century, liturgical renewal led in a few places to recovery of other functions: usually reading the gospel, sometimes saying intercessory prayers or leading the general confession. These deacons functioned mainly as assistant ministers of the word.

Then came the restoration of the permanent diaconate in the Roman Catholic Church. About the same time, the

American Episcopal Church began to experience a revival of diverse ministries and to experiment with rites that made full use of deacons and other persons. Carefully revised, these rites formed the heart of the Book of Common Prayer published in 1979.

Two other volumes provide additions to the prayer book. *The Book of Occasional Services* (BOS) is an official supplement containing seasonal, pastoral, and episcopal liturgies (Church Hymnal, 1994). *The Prayer Book Office*, compiled and edited by Howard E. Galley (Seabury, 1988) gives permissible directions and additions to the daily office.

The liturgies of the Anglican Church of Canada use deacons in ways similar to the American church. The Canadian church published *The Book of Alternative Services* (BAS) in 1985 and a supplemental volume, *Occasional Celebrations*, in 1992.

Deacons, presiders, and other planners of liturgy may use this book along with Howard E. Galley's *Ceremonies of the Eucharist: A Guide to Celebration* (Cowley, 1989), which covers all the aspects, including all the ministers, of the eucharistic liturgy. Another recent manual is Byron D. Stuhlman's *Prayer Book Rubrics Expanded* (Church Hymnal, 1987). Three books by Leonel L. Mitchell provide guides for the seasons and feasts of the Christian year: *Planning the Church Year* (Morehouse, 1991), and *Lent, Holy Week, Easter*, and *The Great Fifty Days* (Cowley, 1996).

This book has several purposes: To help deacons serve in the liturgy with grace and manners, sensitive to the needs of the presider and the people; to help communities of faith use their deacons in ways appropriate to the dignity and meaning of the order; to help communities without the diaconate discover how deacons enhance the liturgy; to help all Christians—bishops, presbyters, deacons, and all the baptized—express baptismal ministry in the life and worship of the church.

1

General Norms

Ordinary Functions of Deacons

Deacons are the principal helpers, the most active of all who serve in the liturgy. They are heralds of the word, servants of the church, and agents of the bishop. At the ordination of a deacon, the bishop tells the ordinand: "You are to assist the bishop and priests in public worship and in the ministration of God's word and sacraments" (BCP 543, BAS 655). The presence of deacons, however, goes beyond mere assistance. It imparts a special quality that rises to the level of symbol. Deacons act for the good of others by setting them free for worship of God and action in the world.

As symbols, deacons embody two ancient concepts, angels and servants. They are messengers and heralds of the word. They proclaim the good news of God in Christ and interpret the world to the community of faith. They wait on table, prepare, serve, and clean up. They enable the hungry to eat and the thirsty to drink. Both angel and servant appear in every deacon in every diaconal function in every liturgy.

Deacons' functions in liturgy reflect their roles outside the liturgy. The bishop presides in all liturgies because the bishop presides in the diocese, and the presbyter presides in the eucharist and other parochial liturgies because the presbyter presides in the parish. Deacons serve in liturgy because deacons mobilize the church, especially for service in the world.

Service to those in need, especially "the poor, the

sick, the suffering, and the helpless" (BCP 510, BAS 631), is focused in worship through the liturgical words and actions of deacons. In this way, among several ways, the messy world enters into the liturgy and Christian people present it to God. In this way, too, deacons reveal the servanthood of Christ in which the people share. The deacons' role in the liturgy reveals the true nature of deacons as proclaimers and evangelists, messengers and bearers of the good news to the poor, and servants in the image of Christ.

Deacons serve in an assembly of worshipers. Their role involves "a special ministry of servanthood directly under your bishop" (BCP 543, see BAS 655). With good grace they submit to the customs of the parish and the practices of the presbyter. Never competing with others for place and prerogative in liturgy, they enlist and involve other baptized persons in proper liturgical roles, as in pastoral and social ministry.

The liturgical functions of deacons come to us partly by descent from the early church and partly by intelligent reform. The text and rubrics of each rite, especially the eucharist and the ordination of a deacon, clearly reveal the essential or ordinary functions. These occur in two main groups, liturgy of the word and liturgy of the sacrament.

Liturgy of the Word

In all liturgies, deacons proclaim the word of God, assuming the role of angel, messenger, and bearer of good news. They act as:

(1) *Reader of the gospel.* A deacon normally proclaims the gospel reading. There are three main exceptions: (a) In the absence of a deacon functioning liturgically, the presider or an assisting presbyter reads the gospel. (b) Other baptized persons may read or sing the passion gospel on Palm Sunday and Good Friday. (c) When part of a congregation speaks a foreign language,

another person may read the gospel in that tongue (perhaps in addition to the gospel in English).

(2) *Occasional preacher.* Preaching is normally a function of the presider. Bishops and presbyters preach because they are ordained for the task. The bishop may license other baptized persons to preach, and in some places, gifted persons preach by the authority of their baptism. Deacons preach as gifted persons, as agents of the bishop, or as those whose duty is "to make Christ and his redemptive love known" (BCP 543, BAS 655). In some dioceses, the bishop assumes that deacons have a right to preach; in others, the bishop licenses deacons to preach.

(3) *Leader of the prayers of the people.* Deacons are the proper leaders of biddings that invite the people to intercede for those in need. Other baptized persons also may lead. When joined by those who share in a ministry of service, deacons take a major role in the prayers.

(4) *Herald.* Deacons announce, exhort, call to worship, instruct, keep order, and act as master of ceremonies. By overseeing the practical details of worship, they enable presbyters and bishops to preside prayerfully and help the people to take part actively. It is an old custom for deacons to announce the feasts of the church year, and on the holiest of nights, they proclaim the Exsultet.

Liturgy of the Sacrament

In the eucharist, deacons serve the table, the role of chief attendant, butler of the house, and steward of the banquet. They act as:

(1) *Waiter.* Deacons prepare the table, receive, prepare, and place on it the bread and wine, serve the cup, and after the meal, eat and drink the remaining bread and wine (aside from what is to be kept) and cleanse the vessels.

(2) *Steward of the wine.* Standing usually at the

presider's right, a deacon raises the cup during the doxology of the eucharistic prayer and at the invitation to communion. At communion, deacons give the wine. At a large celebration, with several deacons and presbyters, some may serve the bread and some the wine. Other persons licensed by the bishop may give the wine "in the absence of sufficient deacons and priests" (BCP 408); canon law permits them also to give the bread. In many places, other persons give communion with little or no restriction. (The Canadian church allows persons "authorized by the bishop" to give communion, BAS 183.)

(3) *Dismisser.* A deacon ends the liturgy by telling the people to go or inviting them to "bless the Lord." The dismissal is part of a deacon's angelic function of making announcements, exhorting, and aiding the active participation of the people.

(4) *Minister of the reserved sacrament.* After ordination a new deacon has the privilege of carrying the reserved sacrament "to those communicants who, because of sickness or other grave cause, could not be present" (BCP 555). (The Canadian church omits the provision.) Deacons also oversee the work of lay eucharistic ministers. Many parishes reserve the sacrament in an aumbry or tabernacle. For easy access during the week, deacons may reserve it at home in a safe place, marked by a lamp or icon. It is customary to keep the sacrament under the form of bread, easy to carry and give, but the wine also may be reserved. Deacons and other ministers carry the bread in a small metal box called a pyx (Latin *pyxis* or box). They may carry the wine in a small bottle, or intinct the bread in the wine before taking it to communicants.

Deacons and the Bishop

In all ordinary functions, deacons act as emissaries and deputies of the bishop. From Ignatius of Antioch at the beginning of the second century, deacons have stood in a special relationship to the bishop. At the ordination, the bishop tells the deacon-elect: "God now calls you to a special ministry of servanthood directly under your bishop" (BCP 543, see BAS 655). Two deacons normally attend the bishop as presider of liturgies. Even if presbyters are present, deacons serve in their proper functions. Deacons especially help the bishop at ordinations. In the rites for investing and seating a diocesan bishop, the normal number of attendants is set at two deacons (BOS 243, 251).

Movement and Gestures of Deacons

In a procession deacons normally walk just ahead of the presider (and concelebrants). If the presider is a bishop, two attending deacons walk a little behind the bishop. In a procession with the paschal candle, a deacon bears the lighted candle and leads the procession (in place of the cross).

The normal seats for deacons are at the presider's right and left. During the liturgy of the word, however, deacons may stay in a position closer to the people. Deacons' seats should be visible and preferably face the people.

During the liturgy of the sacrament, deacons stand and move near the altar. The normal position of deacons during the eucharistic prayer is at the presider's right and left, two or three steps back. They step forward to handle the cup and turn pages. (With the altar book placed on the left, a single deacon may walk to that side as needed to turn pages, unless someone else turns them.)

Except when performing some action, deacons hold hands folded (fingers interlocking) or joined (palm to palm), following the presider's preference. In the early church, during prayer all persons held their hands raised and extended to the side, palms turned forward and upward. When leading the prayers of the people, a deacon may use this *orans* or prayer gesture.

When reading, deacons look at the text. When addressing persons, they look at the persons.

Vestments of Deacons

The distinctive vestments of deacons in the Western church are the alb and dalmatic. Commonly added to these is the stole worn over the left shoulder, originating in the Eastern church.

Deacons wear vestments in all liturgies. At the ordination of a deacon, the deacon-elect wears a surplice or an alb. After the prayer of consecration, the new deacon receives a "stole worn over the left shoulder, or other insignia of the office of deacon" (BCP 536, 554, see BAS 666). This rubric reflects a long and complicated history and a diversity of styles involving alb, dalmatic, and stole.

The alb (Latin *albus* or white) is the white robe originally given to each new Christian at baptism. Worn as an undergarment (the traditional way), the alb is simple, lightweight, and girded by a rope; it may include a hood or neckband or a separate neckpiece, the amice (Latin *amictus* or mantle). Worn as an outer garment, the alb is heavier, elegant in fabric and cut, and ungirded; it may reach the dimensions of a dalmatic with a hood and wide sleeves. In the frigid buildings of northern Europe, wearing heavy garments under the alb eventually turned that ancient dress into a surplice (Latin *superpellicium* or overcoat).

The "other insignia" is the dalmatic (originally a tunic of white Dalmatian wool), the outer garment of deacons in the Western church. (Eastern deacons wear the *sticharion,* a colorful, textured tunic.) Like all other vestments, the dalmatic degenerated over the centuries. In the late Middle Ages deacons wore an ornate dalmatic in the color of the day, open at the sides, with the stole underneath.

In many places today, the medieval style has given way to the primitive dalmatic. This garment is an ample white or off-white tunic, simple, sober, and functional, often with the stole on top. The early dalmatic included wide sleeves with bands about the cuffs and *clavi,* or colored bands, descending from the shoulders to the hem. The design of dalmatics and other vestments ought to reflect local culture as well as ancient tradition. When handmade of natural fabrics, vestments show our concern for the beauty and preservation of God's creation.

Deacons may wear a dalmatic at all celebrations of the eucharist and on other solemn occasions including evensong. A good rule of thumb is: when the presider wears a chasuble or cope, the deacons wear a dalmatic.

The stole (Latin *stola* or garment) is an insignia of office. It may have begun in the East as an ornate toga, folded and drawn about the body, which degenerated into a scarf. In the Eastern church the stole is called *orarion* (Latin *orare,* to speak or to pray), signifying proclamation of the gospel and leadership of intercessory prayer. Like the wings of a cherub or seraph, the eastern deacon wraps orarion over sticharion. The stole flutters, and when chanting a litany the deacon holds one end in three fingers of the right hand, like a folded wing.

Deacons wear the stole over the left shoulder in three ways:

(1) Ends tied or attached under the right arm. In the late classical age, western deacons added the eastern stole to the Roman dalmatic, wearing it on top. An eleventh century miniature, codex 73 of the library at Monte Cassino, shows Peter (archdeacon to Gregory the Great) wearing his stole over his dalmatic; it hangs straight down from the left shoulder. Later, when deacons wore the stole under the dalmatic, they tied the ends to keep them out of the way.

(2) Straight down from the left shoulder. As in the picture of deacon Peter, this style may be the primitive use. Parish deacons in Russia and a few other places in the East still wear the orarion hanging straight. To stay put, the fabric needs to be heavy or rough, or deacons may use a patch of velcro on the shoulder.

(3) Wrapped about the body. In the so-called Byzantine style, deacons wear a long stole with the middle under the right arm and the ends hanging from the left shoulder. This vestment is the double orarion, originally two stoles sewed end to end. Russian archdeacons and protodeacons wear it as a mark of dignity. The style spread to the Greek church, where all deacons now wear the double orarion.

Crosses and similar ornaments are personal adornments, worn underneath vestments. Before the liturgy deacons ought to remove their wristwatches, which distract the people and underscore the passage of time. In place of the obsolescent maniple, at the offertory or communion deacons may drape a large white towel over their left wrist. While cleansing the vessels, they may hang it over their left shoulder.

In the absence of a deacon, assisting presbyters who perform diaconal functions vest as priests, to avoid being mistaken for deacons. It is also confusing for anyone to vest as subdeacon, an order abolished in 1550.

Books of Deacons

The altar book, designed as a sacramentary for the presider, also contains texts and chants for deacons. Special books are desirable for the gospels and the prayers of the people:

(1) *Book of gospels.* Before the Reformation, deacons received a book of gospels at their ordination. This ancient tradition of the instruments became lost in post-Reformation Anglicanism, replaced by the giving

of a New Testament. It remains lost in the Episcopal church with the giving of a Bible (given also to new bishops and presbyters). For the eucharistic lessons and gospels, the prayer book now encourages the use of "a book or books of appropriate size and dignity" (BCP 406, BAS 183). This rubric has led to the publication in several versions of a book of gospels, impressively bound in metal or leather. These contain either gospel pericopes for Sundays, major feasts, and other days, or the entire text of the four gospels.

(2) *Book of intercessions.* The *diaconicon* or diaconal, used only in Eastern churches, contains all the deacon's parts in the liturgy. Modern deacons may compile their own diaconal, including prayers of the people for weekly, seasonal, and occasional use.

Music of Deacons

Deacons may sing all the texts assigned them, except for personal parts such as the words at communion. Liturgical chant elevates the text and brings out the meaning. The chants appointed in the altar book are based on ancient melodies. The official chants are melodically simple and generous to singers of limited voice. Deacons should sing them in an unhurried and dignified manner, with respect for the rhythm and meaning of the words.

Deacons' chants are:

(1) *Gospel.* The altar book provides two tones, which deacons apply to the appointed gospel. Tone I is the Sarum form of an early melody. It consists of a reciting note with cadences or ending melodies at the metrum (major pause within a sentence), punctum (end of sentence), question, and conclusion. Tone II dates from the late sixteenth century. It is simpler, omitting the cadence at the metrum. The people's responses are the same for both tones. Other traditional tones are also available, and deacons may compose their own

chants. One way to introduce gospel-chant to a congregation is to sing only the announcement and ending, enabling the people to sing their responses (unaccompanied).

(2) *Prayers of the people.* For the eucharist, the altar book and hymnal provide chants for forms I and V (S 106 and 109), singable and appropriate for regular Sunday and festal use. Each form has two tones, derived from Gregorian and Ambrosian sources. Tones for other forms are in the hymnal (III at S 107, IV at S 108) and its service music supplement (II at S 362, VI at S 363). A deacon sings the solemn intercessions of Good Friday to the simple preface tone. After each bidding the deacon may sing, "Let us kneel in silent prayer," and "Arise." The versicles and litanies in the daily office have their own chants. For other special and occasional litanies, a deacon may use traditional or modern formulas involving a reciting note with ending cadence.

(3) *Dismissal.* For ordinary dismissals, the altar book and hymnal provide a simple formula based on Gregorian chant (S 174). For the Easter dismissal (with two alleluias), they give the traditional Roman chant (S 175). In some plainchant mass settings, the dismissal repeats the *Kyrie* melody.

(4) *Processions.* The altar book and hymnal provide the versicle tone for "Let us go forth in peace" on Palm Sunday (service music supplement S 342) and "The light of Christ" at the Easter Vigil (S 68). Other processions with diaconal chants (as on Candlemas) may use similar chants.

(5) *Exsultet.* Originally deacons composed their own paschal proclamations, but by the seventh century the present form came into being in northern Italy. Differences in melodic treatment distinguish the introductory or "Rejoice" stanzas, with their lyric quality, from the formal blessing of the candle, a recitation in the solemn

preface tone. Deacons may use other chants, and those with limited voice may simply sing the Exsultet to a monotone with slight inflections.

(6) *Prayers for the candidates.* For the baptismal litany, the altar book provides a litany tone from Gregorian tradition.

2

Deacons in Christian Initiation

A person who desires to become a Christian passes from death to life and enters a new family. This pastoral, social, and liturgical passage takes place in the company of parents, godparents, sponsors, and the entire supporting Christian community. Deacons reveal proclamation and service and guide the new Christian through darkness and perilous waters. Purged of sin and death, washed in the blood of the Lamb, and sealed by the Spirit, the new Christian follows deacons bearing the light of Christ into a new fellowship of brothers and sisters.

The church provides a short and a long form for Christian initiation: (1) Holy Baptism (suitable for both adults and children) and (2) the Catechumenate, ending in Holy Baptism (suitable only for adults, or those mature enough to receive instruction). The church also provides a means for mature baptized persons to prepare to reaffirm their baptismal covenant (see chapter 6).

Holy Baptism

At a normal celebration of baptism, within the eucharist, deacons proclaim the gospel reading, lead intercessions, serve at the altar, and otherwise help. Especially, a deacon:

(1) Leads the procession to the font, bearing the lighted paschal candle (unless it is already near the font). The deacon continues to hold the candle. At the

Easter Vigil the deacon usually hands the candle to the presider, who dips it into the water during the solemn blessing.

(2) May lead the prayers for the candidates. Although the prayer book suggests a sponsor for the role (BCP 312, BAS 163), a deacon is also a proper litanist, especially when more than one of them is present. A deacon may sing or say the petitions during the procession to the font.

(3) May baptize, by immersion or pouring. After the presider has blessed the water, several different ministers may baptize different candidates. Each baptizer—presider, assisting presbyter, or deacon—is appropriately the one who has prepared, or helped to prepare, the candidate or parents.

(4) Lights a candle from the paschal candle and hands it to the newly baptized or, with infants and younger children, to a parent or godparent.

(5) Bearing the paschal candle, leads the way back to the chancel for chrismation and reception of the newly baptized.

6) Helps to give first communion to the newly baptized, completing Christian initiation.

On a few exceptional occasions, a deacon presides in baptism. If a bishop or presbyter is unavailable at the Easter Vigil or on the Day of Pentecost, All Saints' Day or the Sunday following, or the feast of the Baptism of our Lord, "the bishop may specially authorize a deacon to preside." The deacon must omit everything that follows the water baptism. Since this liturgy truncates Christian initiation, the church must supply the omitted parts later at a "public baptism at which a bishop or priest presides" (BCP 312). (The Canadian church allows the deacon to include everything, BAS 163.)

Parents and godparents "are to be instructed in the meaning of Baptism, in their duties to help the new Christian grow in the knowledge and love of God, and in their responsibilities as members of his Church" (BCP 298, BAS 150). In this preparation, deacons "have a special role as leaders of servant ministry" (BOS 157). The preparation of mature candidates properly occurs in the context of the catechumenate.

The Catechumenate and Holy Baptism

The catechumenate is a period of integration and enlightenment for adults who wish to become Christians. Details of the period, including its liturgies, appear in *The Book of Occasional Services,* pp. 112–26. "Traditionally, the preparation of catechumens is a responsibility of the bishop, which is shared with the presbyters, deacons, and appointed lay catechists of the diocese" (BOS 112). The catechumenate consists of three stages leading up to baptism, followed by a fourth period. It is normal for deacons to minister in all four stages.

(1) *The pre-catechumenal period.* Deacons may conduct inquiry classes and otherwise help inquirers decide whether they want to become Christians. A deacon may name the inquirers in the prayers of the people.

(2) *The catechumenate.* Deacons may instruct catechumens in the Christian life, prayer, and scripture. A sponsor (who may be a deacon) accompanies each catechumen through the process. Especially, deacons lead and encourage catechumens in care of the poor, the weak, the sick, and the lonely, and show them that in serving the helpless they serve Christ.

The stage begins with a rite of admission of catechumens, in the midst of the Sunday liturgy. The sponsors mark a cross on the foreheads of their catechumens. In the prayers of the people, a deacon mentions the new catechumens by name. During the stages of catechumenate and candidacy, at each formal teaching session the instructor—"whether bishop, priest, deacon, or lay catechist"—concludes by praying over the catechumens and then "by laying a hand individually on the head of each catechumen in silence" (BOS 117).

(3) *Candidacy for baptism.* The stage normally co-incides with Lent, with baptism at the Easter Vigil. (It may also occur in the incarnational cycle, with baptism on the feast of our Lord's Baptism.) The stage includes a rite of enrollment of candidates for baptism, after the creed on the first Sunday in Lent. The sponsors appear with their catechumens and may join them in signing the book of enrollment. For the prayers of the people, the deacon "or other person appointed" leads a special litany (BOS 122). On several Sundays during the stage, the candidates continue to come before the presider for special prayers and blessings and the laying on of hands. A deacon adds the names of candidates and sponsors to the prayers of the people.

In some places, following ancient practice, a dea-con dismisses the catechumens and candidates after the homily (or Nicene Creed). In a typical formula, the dea-con sings or says: "Let us pray in silence for the cate-chumens as they prepare to receive the wisdom of the Holy Spirit in baptism." After a period of silent prayer, the deacon continues: "Catechumens, go in peace." The catechumens leave with their sponsors and cate-chists to meet apart, for study and prayer, during the rest of the eucharist. The sponsors and catechists re-turn for communion.

When baptism occurs at the Great Vigil of Easter, as is normal, deacons function as usual. A deacon sponsoring a candidate also acts as sponsor. A deacon with a close relationship as either instructor or sponsor may baptize the candidate. Galley, pp. 231–32, pro-vides a model form for the prayers of the people at baptism and confirmation.

The period after baptism, commonly called *mysta-gogia* (initiation into mysteries), extends through the fifty days of Easter. Less strictly defined than the catechumenate, the period involves integration into the life and worship of the church. Instructors and sponsors continue to help the new Christians. In the broadest sense, Christians live in *mystagogia* the rest of their lives, as they continue to learn the mysteries of Christ's death and resurrection.

3

Deacons in the Eucharist

In the eucharist deacons proclaim the good news of Christ's death and resurrection. They bring the needs, concerns, and hopes of the world into the marriage feast of the Lamb. They feed the hungry and give drink to the thirsty. By exercising a role that illuminates the mystery of Christ and his church, they serve both the people and the Lord.

Although only one bishop or presbyter presides in the eucharist, it is appropriate to have two and sometimes more deacons. If only one deacon serves, this one performs all the functions of deacon. Two deacons may serve in a typical parish liturgy, and as many as three or four when the bishop presides.

Two deacons share duties, usually one on each side of the presider. In a common arrangement, the right or chief deacon reads the gospel and dismisses; the left deacon leads the prayers of the people and the confession of sin. At the offertory, the left deacon helps the right, and the right deacon censes the people. During the eucharistic prayer, both stand back a few steps; the left deacon turns pages, and the right deacon lifts the cup. Both receive communion from the presider, both give the wine (and bread), and both consume the remaining elements and cleanse the vessels.

Unless a bishop presides (see below), other deacons serve mainly as ministers of communion.

All those with leading roles prepare carefully for the

celebration, praying and rehearsing the texts they are to sing or say. Deacons mark the books of the liturgy, wash their hands, vest early, and oversee the preparations of others. They enforce silence in the vesting room. With others, they may say a prayer or office of preparation. Finally, standing at the ambo or other convenient place, a deacon may introduce the eucharist of the day, make necessary announcements, and rehearse the people in a new hymn or the psalm refrain.

The Entrance or Gathering

A deacon carries the book of gospels (held at chest level or high enough for all to see) and enters just ahead of the other deacons, concelebrants (if any), and presider. The deacon immediately places the book, closed and lying flat, on the center of the altar. All bow together.

Christians reverence the altar on entering and leaving. The normal reverence in Anglican practice is a deep bow from the waist. A single genuflection before and after the liturgy is also common when the reserved sacrament is present. In some places, after bowing to the altar, the presider and deacons turn and bow to the people, who also bow. Where it is the custom, the presider and deacons also kiss the altar.

Censing the altar, if used, usually occurs during the entrance hymn. A thurifer brings the censer to the presider. A deacon takes the boat and opens it, and the presider places incense on the coals. The deacon returns the boat to the thurifer, takes the censer, and passes it to the presider. The deacon places the top of the chains in the presider's left hand, the bottom of the chains in the right hand. Usually, the presider censes an altar by walking around it, swinging the censer. The presider hands the censer back to the deacon, who returns it to the thurifer.

During the rest of the entrance rite, at the chair, a

deacon may hold the altar book for the presider, unless an acolyte does this.

The entrance rite may include several options: (1) In the penitential order, a deacon invites the people to confess and, after a period of silence, leads them in confession. (2) In the Great Litany, a deacon may sing or say the petitions, kneeling, standing, or in procession. (3) In the order of worship for the evening, a deacon may light the candles and help with incense. (4) During the fifty days of Easter, if the presider sprinkles the people with water (usually after the collect for purity), deacons may help with water and sprinkler.

There are two other basic forms of gathering for liturgy:

(1) As in the early church, the people gather as one body in the room of celebration, without the ministerial party entering in procession while all stand. A deacon informally places the gospel book on the altar. Each person, including the ministers, bows separately on entering and takes a seat. A deacon may introduce the eucharist of the day, make announcements, and conduct a rehearsal with a hymn or psalm refrain. After a brief period of silence, the presider stands and begins the liturgy.

(2) As at the Easter Vigil (in many places), the people enter as one body into church. Deacons may organize the procession in the parish hall, make announcements, and conduct a rehearsal. A deacon may direct: "Let us go forth in peace." Deacons and presider lead the way, with other ministers, and the liturgy begins as usual.

The Liturgy of the Word

After the collect of the day, while ministers read the lessons and chant the gradual psalm, all others sit. A deacon may monitor the silence after each reading and give a discreet signal when it is to end.

Proclamation of the Gospel

The deacon who is to read the gospel prepares carefully by studying it, practicing it aloud, and absorbing it as prayer.

In a simple weekday liturgy, the deacon may read the gospel without adornment. On Sundays and major feasts, the assembly adorns the gospel with signs of honor. Because the proclamation of the gospel marks the high point of the liturgy of the word, its ceremony is often long and elaborate. Two lights accompany the book of gospels to the place of reading. Some parishes burn incense. In some places the deacon chants the gospel.

Immediately after the second reading, the assembly observes a period of silence. After the silence, or toward the end of the sequence hymn, the deacon and others rise to prepare for the gospel procession. The candlebearers take up their torches. An acolyte brings the censer, if used, to the presider, as before.

The blessing of the deacon is an old custom. The deacon bows low and quietly asks the presider: "[Sir or Madam or N.], give me your blessing." The presider makes the sign of the cross or, in a scriptural form of blessing, lays hands on the deacon's head. The presider says one of two forms of blessing. The first is: "The Lord be in your heart and on your lips that you may worthily proclaim his gospel: In the name of the Father, and of the Son, and of the Holy Spirit." The second is: "May the Spirit of the Lord be upon you as you bring good news to the poor." The first is a translation from the current Roman missal; the second, a paraphrase of Luke 4:18, comes from the Bobbio missals in northern Italy in the tenth and eleventh centuries. The deacon responds "Amen" and turns to join the procession.

The deacon goes before the altar, bows low, and takes up the book. Preceded by (thurifer and) candlebearers, the deacon holds the book high and walks reverently to the place of reading. During the procession, in some places, the choir or people sing an alleluia or (in Lent) tract. In places without these chants, the people finish the sequence hymn. The people turn toward the deacon or even, space permitting, crowd around.

The procession moves to a prominent place. "It is desirable that the Lessons be read from a lectern or pulpit, and that the Gospel be read from the same lectern, or from the pulpit, or from the midst of the congregation" (BCP 406, BAS 183). The third option began in the 1950s as a sign of Christ proclaimed in the world. In a large space, many persons may be unable to see or hear the deacon. Use of a lectern (sometimes called ambo) or pulpit for the entire liturgy of the word makes it possible for all to see and hear. It also emphasizes the unity of the word of God.

At a lectern or pulpit, the deacon places the book on the stand. In the midst of the congregation, the deacon or someone else holds the book.

The deacon opens the book and announces the reading, making a sign of the cross with the right thumb on the book (opening word), forehead, lips, and breast. (In the Canadian church, the deacon first greets the people with "The Lord be with you.") If incense is used, the deacon censes the book with three swings, center, left, right. The deacon sings or says the gospel in a slow and stately manner. At the end of the reading, the deacon pauses briefly and adds: "The gospel of the Lord." It is unnecessary to elevate the book. The deacon may kiss the opening word, saying quietly: "May the words of the gospel wipe away our sins."

When the deacon sings at least the opening and closing formulas, the people are able to sing their response. Today, few deacons sing the entire gospel. If God has given a gift of song to this person, however, the assembly ought to ask the deacon to use it, at least at Christmas and Easter.

Unless the deacon leaves the book of gospels on a lectern or pulpit, the deacon takes the closed book and leads the procession back to the chancel. The deacon places the book on the altar (where it remains until the kiss of peace) or on a side table.

A deacon who is to preach remains in place while the others return to the chancel. It is better to gesture (palms down) than to ask the people to sit. When everyone has settled down, the deacon begins immediately, without announcements, invocation, prayer, or greetings such as "Good morning." The deacon concludes simply or with a doxology. After the homily, there may be a brief period of silence. The deacon may lead the people by beginning the Nicene Creed.

Leading the General Intercessions

Near the end of the creed, a deacon goes to a suitable place for (announcements and) the prayers of the people.

By leading the general intercessions, deacons interpret to the church the needs, concerns, and hopes of the world and help the people respond to them. They suggest topics and invite the people to pray; the people offer petitions to God.

The prayer book provides several models of intercession: the form for Rite One (BCP 328–30) and the six forms suggested for general use (BCP 383–93). (The Canadian church provides nineteen models, BAS 110–28.) They are examples, not standard forms for regular use. A parish may change them, compose new forms, or adapt other forms for every Sunday and feast, the seasons of the church year, or special occasions.

To compose or adapt the intercessions, the deacons may work with other parish leaders who help poor, sick, and needy persons. It is desirable to have someone skilled in writing perform the actual drafting.

In designing intercessions, drafters ought to follow six principles:

First, the intercessions must include six categories: the church, the world, the nation, the community, the suffering, and the dead. Biddings may cover them in full on Sundays and major feasts and condense them on weekdays and other occasions.

Second, the intercessions are *general.* They ask God's mercy on all those in need in the church and the world. Specific names and local concerns ought to be used with restraint. Except on special occasions, such as weddings and funerals, it is better to announce special intentions before the intercessions. It is an ancient custom, however, to include the name of the bishop in the formal biddings.

Third, they are *intercessions,* prayers primarily for the relief of needs, the remedy of concerns, and the fulfillment of hopes. It is better to leave praise and thanksgiving to other parts of the liturgy.

Fourth, the intercessions are prayers of the *people.* A deacon as leader normally addresses the people, who do the actual praying. Although several forms in the prayer book have the leader invoke God in terms such as "Father, we pray," invocation is suitable mainly when other baptized persons function as leaders. When others lead, they act as priests, standing for the assembly. When deacons lead, they act as heralds, reminding the people of topics and asking them to pray, and the people intercede through silence or responses.

Fifth, the biddings or intentions are normally short and easy to follow. Brief, simple biddings help the people to grasp the topic. Biddings may begin with a formula such as "For [persons or concerns]" or "That [intention]." These may be combined as "For [persons or concerns], that [intention]." Biddings may end abruptly or, to prompt the response, with a cue such as "let us pray to the Lord." A sensible number is four to six biddings on weekdays, and nine to twelve on Sundays and major feasts.

Sixth, the responses are normally brief, uniform, and easy to remember. Long or variable responses require the people to read from a book or paper. Short ones allow them to look up and see the deacon and each other, the altar, an icon, and other aids to prayer. They are free to hold hands or raise them in prayer.

The presider, deacon, or committee may also adapt or compose the brief invitation and the concluding collect or doxology. These usually reflect the occasion, season, or day. The presider needs a copy of the text.

There are two main places to lead the prayers: (1) At the lectern or pulpit, the deacon faces the people. (2) In the midst or at the head of the congregation, the deacon may begin by facing the people (or by facing away from the altar). After "In peace, let us pray to the Lord," or some other opening phrase, the deacon turns to face the altar (as in the Eastern church).

The choice of a place should suit the worship space and the needs of the congregation. The people may form a circle around the altar. They may focus on an icon or some other point of prayer. Or they may stand where they are. The presider may stand on one side of the assembly (the *east* side) or at the chair. The deacon may stand on the opposite side, or among the people, or at an ambo.

After the presider's invitation, the deacon may read, or arrange for others to read, a few special intentions of the catholic church, the diocese, and the parish. These may include the Anglican and diocesan cycles of prayer. Local intentions may include baptism days, wedding anniversaries, the sick, and the dead. For this purpose, leaders may use a large book of weekly remembrances, with blank pages for the names.

After the special intentions, the deacon may invite the people to recall their daily prayers and offer their own names and concerns silently or aloud. After giving them a little time (but not long), the deacon begins the formal biddings.

While singing or saying the biddings, the deacon keeps hands folded or extends them in the *orans* or prayer gesture. (The prayer gesture is suitable when the deacon is facing the altar.) To hold the prayer gesture, the deacon may need to memorize the biddings, or someone else may hold a book containing the text. During the prayers the deacon or a server may gently swing a censer, with "much incense to mingle with the prayers of all the saints" (Rev. 8:3).

When the intercessions take the form of a litany, it is often desirable to sing them. The leader sings either the whole bidding or the ending phrase. (If necessary, someone else sings the ending.) The people sing their response either in unison or in harmony. They may overlap a response such as "Lord, have mercy" with the preceding bidding and hum during the following bidding.

Although deacons normally lead the intercessions, they often involve other baptized persons in the performance. Others may announce special intentions beforehand, lead some of the biddings, say different parts of biddings, or share the leadership in some other way. If they minister to those in need in the church and the world, their leadership in the prayers of the people will convey authority.

At the end, after a period of silence, the presider extends hands and concludes with a collect or doxology.

If the people confess their sins just before the peace, a deacon says the invitation and, after a period of silence long enough to recollect sins, begins the confession.

If the people are slow to rise for the peace, a deacon may gesture for them to stand (palms up). After the presider has given the peace, a deacon may announce, "Greet one another with a sign of peace," or give a similar direction (even singing it, if the presider has sung the peace). Then the deacons greet the presider and others nearby, according to local custom. The formal greeting in the Western church is a light embrace cheek to cheek.

Before the offertory, a deacon may make other necessary announcements. These should be brief and help the liturgy move to the next action.

The Liturgy of the Sacrament

As in the ancient church, preparation of the table and of the bread and wine is the proper function of deacons. The common name of the action is *offertory,* from the people's offerings of bread and wine and other gifts. Another acceptable title is *preparation.*

The Preparation of the Table and the Gifts

When the prayer book speaks of what a deacon does in the preparation, it uses domestic language, words of kitchen and dining room, ordinary food and drink, and a festive table where people gather to eat. A deacon "make[s] ready the Table for the celebration, preparing and placing upon it the bread and cup of wine," to which it is customary "to add a little water" (for sobriety, originally) (BCP 407, see BAS 183).

When the prayer book speaks of what the presider and people do, it uses temple language, words of sacrifice, offering, and altar. Members of the assembly bring to the deacon "the people's offerings of bread and wine, and money or other gifts." They "are presented and placed on the Altar" (BCP 333, 361, see BAS 192).

To describe the action another way, in the liturgy of the sacrament, deacons and other liturgical helpers function as servants, while the presider and the rest of the people function as priests. Servants wait on table, priests offer sacrifice. Deacons set free and enable others to act at the highest level of their baptismal role, sharing in the royal and eternal priesthood of Christ.

Throughout the preparation, the presider remains at the chair. Deacons and other persons help the chief deacon. The action involves four distinct steps:

(1) *Preparing the table.* A deacon brings an empty paten or dish and one chalice or cup to the table, places them to one side (usually the right), and spreads a large white cloth known as the corporal. The cloth was originally what we now call the "fair linen," covering the entire top of the table. It makes sense to go back to early usage and leave the table uncovered until the preparation.

The prayer book requires "only one chalice on the Altar, and, if need be, a flagon of wine for filling additional chalices after the Breaking of the Bread" (BCP 407, see BAS 184). The reason for one chalice lies in scriptural and traditional evidence of one cup (and one bread) as a sign of unity. The deacon sets the dish and cup on the right, alongside the cloth.

In some places, persons bring up the bread already on a dish, or a loaf in a basket, to be used on the table. The deacon prepares the table with only a cup.

The deacon places a purificator or hand towel on the right side. A burse and veil are unnecessary.

(2) *Receiving the gifts.* One or two deacons stand either behind the table or in front of it, at the center. Members of the congregation bring, in this order, special offerings (such as food for the hungry), money, and bread and wine. They present them directly to the deacons, who place them on the table or nearby. Special gifts go probably nearby, money on the right corner of the table (removed just before the eucharistic prayer), bread and wine to the right of the dish and cup.

(3) *Preparing the gifts.* Standing behind the table, at the center, the chief deacon puts the bread on the dish. A second deacon pours sufficient wine in the cup

and adds a little water to the wine in the cup and in any flagons, decanters, or other containers to remain on the table. An acolyte usually helps by bringing water and taking away unneeded vessels.

(4) *Placing the gifts.* The chief deacon places the vessels on the cloth. The dish goes on the left, and the cup on the right. The reasons for this positioning are both ancient and practical. In the early church, the bishop was often old, the bread dish large, and the wine bowl a heavy amphora with two handles. At certain points the bishop raised the bread, sometimes with help, and a deacon, usually younger, raised the wine bowl. Deacons also needed to keep insects from the wine (hence the large fans still used in some eastern liturgies). Today, placing the vessels side by side makes them visible to the congregation and emphasizes the centrality of worship around one altar.

Flagons and other wine containers usually go on the right, or sometimes on either side, allowing the people to see the dish and cup. They may have to be placed off the cloth.

When all is ready, the deacons step aside and the bishop or presbyter comes to the altar for censing (if used), washing hands, and the great thanksgiving.

The rite of censing helps the assembly to lay aside earthly cares and gather prayerfully for the mystery about to take place. The right deacon helps the presider, who puts incense on the coals, censes the bread and wine, and circles the altar. The presider hands the censer to the deacon. The deacon then censes the people, either with three swings for each group or walking among them and censing continuously. (It is customary to bow deeply before and after censing persons and objects.) The deacon censes groups of persons as a body and treats bishops, presbyters, and other baptized persons as equals. The deacon hands the censer to the thurifer, who censes the deacon. (Alternatively, after the deacon has censed the presider, the thurifer censes the deacon and the people.)

For the lavabo or washing of hands, a deacon or an acolyte goes to the presider with a towel over the left arm, a bowl in the left hand, and a pitcher of water in the right hand. Someone takes away the money or other gifts. Finally, a deacon or an acolyte places the book on the left side of the altar, open to the beginning of the eucharistic prayer.

The Eucharistic Prayer

Inconspicuous but ready, two deacons stand a few steps behind the presider during the eucharistic prayer, normally to the right and left. The right deacon attends to the wine, the left deacon the book. (A single deacon stands on the right and moves as needed to turn pages and lift the cup.) If insects are present, the right deacon covers and uncovers the cup with a pall or folded cloth. If the presider bows at "Holy, holy, holy," the deacons also bow. At the beginning of the final doxology, the right deacon steps to the altar and lifts the cup, while the presider lifts the bread, replaces it after "Amen," and steps back. Then the deacons bow deeply, while the presider bows or genuflects.

In each eucharistic prayer, the invitation to the memorial acclamation is addressed to God and belongs to the presider. Because the intercessions in prayer D are in the form of prayer, the presider normally says them; on a special occasion such as the feast of All Saints or the Sunday after, a deacon may read a list of the parish dead.

The Breaking of the Bread

The presider breaks the loaf in two and prays silently. During this period of silence, or later, a deacon may quietly say:

Wisdom has built her house,
she has mixed her wine,
she has set her table.
Glory to you, O God, for ever.

(Although Galley, p. 162, suggests that deacons use the prayer after filling the additional cups, at that point they often are busy with other preparations. The text, partly from Proverbs 9:1–2, was proposed as an offertory prayer in the first draft of the new Roman rite.)

While the presider (and others) continue to break the bread, during the fraction anthem, deacons bring additional dishes and cups, as needed, to the altar and fill the cups from the flagons. "In the absence of a sufficient number of priests, deacons may assist in the Bread-breaking" (BOS 15).

The Communion

When the presider, lifting the bread, says the invitation to communion, the right deacon lifts the cup. Before the presider eats the bread and drinks the wine, the deacon quietly says the words of administration. (Since all the people of God are to receive communion, in some places deacons give communion to the presider.) After the presider's (and concelebrants') communion, the deacons receive the sacrament in both kinds, standing. The other eucharistic ministers then communicate, and after them, the people.

Normally, deacons and lay eucharistic ministers give the cup, following the presider along a line of communicants, or standing at a suitable distance from the presider at a station. After saying the communion sentence, deacons allow each communicant time to say "Amen" before giving the cup. Now that many persons are receiving in the ancient posture of standing, deacons ought to encourage them to grasp the bowl and take the cup. Young children may need help, and in-

fants may have to suck wine from the deacon's or a
parent's finger.

"When several deacons or priests are present,
some may administer the Bread and others the Wine"
(BCP 408, see BAS 666). Lay eucharistic ministers
also may give the bread. Deacons may fill cups from
flagons and otherwise help the other ministers. The
presider, if elderly or ill or simply in need of rest and
prayer, may sit down and let others give communion.

Because of communicable illness or other sound
reason, some persons prefer to receive the sacrament
"in both kinds simultaneously, in a manner approved
by the bishop" (BCP 408). The manner usually means
intinction, or dipping bread in wine, either by the deacon or by the communicant. Some persons, including
young children, prefer to receive only the bread.

If not already seated, the presider goes to the chair
after communion. Deacons take bread and wine for the
communion of the sick and other absent persons. In
many places, lay eucharistic ministers come to the altar
for the same purpose. Deacons give them bread and
wine from the remaining elements (never from the reserved sacrament), and the ministers place them in
pyxes and bottles. In some places, a prayer or statement of purpose accompanies the action. If some of
the sacrament needs to be reserved, a deacon takes
bread (and wine) to the tabernacle or aumbry. (In some
places the taking and reserving of the remaining sacrament occur later.)

Cleaning up after communion is a practical and un-
obtrusive activity. At the ordination of a deacon, "if the
remaining Elements are not required for the Communion of the absent, it is appropriate for the deacons to
remove the vessels from the Altar, consume the remaining Elements, and cleanse the vessels in some
convenient place" (BCP 555, see BAS 184). These
three actions, removing, consuming, and cleansing,

take place usually right after communion (or during the postcommunion prayer or closing hymn). The prayer book also permits them to occur after the dismissal (BCP 409, BAS 184).

It is desirable to consume the remaining bread and wine reverently and in full view of the people. Deacons and others, as needed, consume them at the altar. After eating the bread, they empty the crumbs into the cups and drink the wine. (They may also consume them after removing them from the altar. This alternative is often necessary at diocesan and other large celebrations.)

Deacons and others then remove the vessels to a side table or another room. They rinse the cups with water, which they drink, and wipe them with hand towels. A deacon folds and removes the cloth. Someone removes the altar book, unless the presider is to lead the postcommunion prayer from the altar.

The Dismissal

The deacons go to the presider's side for the (blessing and) dismissal. In Lent, if the presider uses a formal prayer over the people, a deacon first sings or says: "Bow down before the Lord." Hands joined, facing the people, a deacon sings or says the dismissal.

The prayer book gives four formulas. Deacons may use them interchangeably or vary them by theme and season. During the fifty days of Easter, deacons add "alleluia, alleluia" to the dismissal.

Deacons and presider (kiss the altar and) bow deeply to the altar and go out in the same order as they came in. Or they disperse without further ceremony.

Other Forms of Celebration

A community assembled regularly in a church celebrates the normative eucharistic liturgy, typically with presbyter, deacons, cantor, readers, acolytes, and congregation. Deacons also serve in other forms:

(1) *Episcopal.* When the bishop presides, one or two deacons function as usual in the eucharist. It is desirable to have at least three deacons.

When there are only two deacons, both attend the bishop, and the right deacon acts as senior, bearing the gospel book and assisting with the cup. When there are three or more deacons, two attend the bishop, and another acts as senior.

When there are two or more deacons, two attend the bishop, one on each side. Before the liturgy, they vest first and help the bishop to vest. At the entrance, they walk a little behind the bishop. After receiving the miter and pastoral staff, they reverence the altar with the bishop. During the liturgy of the word, the left deacon helps with staff and altar book, and the right deacon holds the miter. Unless other deacons are present (see below), at the altar the left deacon turns pages, and the right deacon lifts the cup. At censings of the altar, both deacons may go with the bishop, the right before and the left after, or they may stand aside. (If the bishop wears a skullcap, one of the deacons removes it before the eucharistic prayer.) Both deacons may assist the bishop in giving communion, at the rail or at a station. After communion, they return to the chair with the bishop. On leaving, they reverence the altar with the bishop.

A senior deacon, if present, bears the gospel book, enters ahead of the other deacons, concelebrants, and bishop with attending deacons, and places the book on the altar. The senior deacon proclaims the gospel reading, leads the intercessions and the confession of sin, prepares the altar and gifts, censes the people, cleans up, and makes announcements (including the dismissal).

A fourth deacon, if present, helps the senior deacon at the altar and leads the intercessions and the confession of sin. Either of these deacons may function as master of ceremonies, vested with dalmatic and stole. Other deacons may give communion.

If concelebrants come to the altar, they need to give the deacons room to help with cup and book.

On occasion, a bishop functions liturgically (for example, as preacher) without presiding. If possible, one or two deacons attend the bishop, remaining nearby.

(2) *Concelebration.* In a form used mainly at ordinations and other diocesan liturgies, and sometimes in parish liturgies, additional presbyters and bishops concelebrate at the altar, or nearby, during the eucharistic prayer. The concelebrants need to be careful to give the deacons room at the altar. Rather than moving aside from time to time, they may remain back in a semicircle until they step forward to join in the breaking of bread.

(3) *Less formal or house liturgies* (home, school, family, and the like). Many parishes hold informal liturgies on occasions such as picnics. A few small congregations lacking a church building meet regularly in houses or other informal places. Wherever they take place, informal liturgies ought to include a diversity of ministries. The nature of the gathering usually calls for careful reduction or alteration in ceremony.

(4) *Holy Communion by a deacon.* Communion by a deacon from the reserved sacrament includes most of the normative liturgy except the offertory, eucharistic prayer, and breaking of the bread. Formerly called *deacon's mass,* the liturgy is for use only in an emergency, when a presbyter is unavailable. The bishop must authorize the service. Its use as a regular liturgy in a congregation, over a long time, tends to distort the nature of ministry and worship. The prayer book outlines the rite on p. 408. (The Canadian church omits the service.)

(5) *Communion from the reserved sacrament.* As

part of their normal ministry, deacons use brief liturgies to give the sacrament to two kinds of communicants:

(a) Those unable to attend the eucharist for a long time. Deacons use the form for Communion under Special Circumstances (BCP 396, BAS 257).

(b) The sick. Deacons also use the form for Communion under Special Circumstances. They may include this form in Ministration to the Sick (BCP 457, BAS 556).

4

Deacons in the Daily Office

At their baptism, all Christians enter a life of prayer, both privately and in community. Deacons swear at their ordination to "be faithful in prayer, and in the reading and study of the holy scriptures" (BCP 544, BAS 655). They fulfill the duty especially in morning and evening prayer. Deacons function in these offices on four levels:

(1) *Private.* If prayer in community is unavailable, deacons pray the daily office privately.

(2) *Family.* Daily prayer in families and other close groups lies at the heart of Christian life. A deacon or other adult may lead, and different persons may take different parts. They may shorten or alter the office.

(3) *Choral.* When a community sings the daily office in choir, in church or elsewhere, it is unnecessary to follow distinctions of order. A deacon functions as officiant or assistant, or simply as member of the choral assembly. In the absolution, an officiating deacon or unordained person substitutes "us" for "you" and "our" for "your" (BCP 42, 63, 80, 117, see BAS). They similarly alter a blessing at the end of worship for the evening (BCP 114). As assistant to a bishop or presbyter, a deacon may read the gospel when it is a lesson and sing the intercessions and dismissal.

(4) *Solemn.* Solemnity includes the use of diverse ministries (bishop or presbyter, deacons, cantor, readers, acolytes), vestments, chant, and incense. Communities

sometimes sing morning prayer solemnly on Sundays
and feasts. More commonly, they sing evensong
solemnly on Saturdays and Sundays, feasts and their
eves, and special occasions. Wearing the dalmatic, one
or two deacons help with incense, chant the litany, and
dismiss the people. Two other deacons attend a bishop
who presides (or is present). At the *Phos hilaron* or
candle-lighting hymn the presider censes the altar by
walking around it.

> The deacon or a server then censes the officiant and
> the people. (If other clergy are present in the sanctu-
> ary, they are censed collectively along with the offi-
> ciant. The bishop of the diocese, however, may be
> censed individually, even if he is not the officiant.)
> No distinction is to be made in the manner of censing
> clergy and lay persons. (*Prayer Book Office* 107)

There may be a second censing of the altar (but not of
the officiant and people) at the *Magnificat* on Easter
Day and on the eves of other feasts of our Lord, with
one or three circuits.

On Easter Day and during its octave, solemn evensong takes an ancient form known as Great Paschal
Vespers, which includes a procession down to the font
and back to the rood or chancel entrance. "If the officiant is a bishop . . . the devotions at the font are led
by a deacon, and those before the cross by a priest. If
the officiant is a priest, the prayers at the font may be
led by a lay reader, and those before the cross by a deacon" (*Prayer Book Office* 360). A deacon also sings a
litany and the Easter dismissal.

The Canadian church allows a deacon or other person to preside at an evening service of light (as a single
service or as an introduction to evensong). The leader
sings or says the opening acclamation and a solemn
thanksgiving over the candle (BAS 61). This long blessing follows Jewish models.

5

Deacons in Seasonal Liturgies

In all seasons of the church year, including Advent and Lent, deacons wear the dalmatic. The prayers of the people may emphasize seasonal themes. (The Canadian church provides four seasonal litanies, BAS 119–22.)

Christmas and Epiphany

Following the example of the Exsultet on Easter, in some places it is customary for a deacon (or someone else) to announce other feasts and seasons. There are two main occasions for this custom.

At midnight mass on Christmas, just before the entrance hymn, a deacon may chant "The Proclamation of Christmas." There is a similar proclamation on Epiphany or the Sunday after, when a deacon may chant "The Announcement of the Date of Easter" after the creed, or in place of it. Accompanied by two candles, the deacon goes to the ambo or other suitable place, and the people stand. Texts and music for these chants appear in the annual *Sourcebook for Sundays and Seasons,* published by Liturgy Training Publications in Chicago.

Candlemas

Immediately before the eucharist, the congregation, after singing *Nunc dimittis,* processes into church carrying lighted candles. To start the procession, a deacon directs "Let us go forth in peace" (BOS 52). A deacon carries the book of gospels. Two deacons attend a bishop who presides or is present.

Ash Wednesday

After the sermon, all standing, a deacon (or the presider) sings or says the invitation to a holy Lent. With others, a deacon may help the presider in the imposition of ashes (BCP 264–65, BAS 281–85). A deacon imposes ashes on the presider. Only the presider leads the litany of penitence, which substitutes for the prayers of the people. Two deacons attend a bishop who presides or is present.

In the absence of a bishop or presbyter, a deacon or licensed person presides at the entire liturgy of the word, including the rite of ashes. For the absolution at the end of the litany, the deacon "remains kneeling and substitutes the prayer for forgiveness appointed at Morning Prayer" (BCP 269, see BAS 286).

Lent

When there are candidates for baptism, a deacon uses a special form of the prayers of the people on the first Sunday in Lent (BOS 122). On all the Sundays of Lent, a deacon names the candidates and sponsors in the intercessions. In place of a blessing, the presider may sing or say a solemn prayer over the people, a deacon first directing: "Bow down before the Lord" (BOS 22).

The Sunday of the Passion: Palm Sunday

In the liturgy of the palms, a deacon proclaims the gospel as usual: asks for and receives a blessing, announces the gospel, censes the book, sings the gospel, and gives the closing. To start the procession to church, a deacon directs: "Let us go forth in peace" (BCP 271, see BAS 299). Two deacons attend a bishop who presides or is present.

"In the absence of a bishop or priest, the preceding service may be led by a deacon or lay reader" (BCP 272, BAS 299).

In ancient times, a deacon alone proclaimed the passion gospel. The practice of using three readers came into use about the fourteenth century. Although a deacon alone may chant the passion gospel, despite its length, it has become common for several other singers, and sometimes the whole congregation, to join in the recitation. The prayer book allows the passion to be "read or chanted by lay persons" (BCP 273, BAS 300). A deacon takes the role of narrator, a second soloist the part of Christ, and a third the other solo parts. All stand at the lectern, ambo, or pulpit. The choir or congregation may perform as the crowd. Those who sing will need the music; the crowd may sing on one note.

The readers recite the passion gospel with a special announcement, without candles and censing, and without congregational responses before and after. At the account of the death of Christ, all kneel in silence (in English usage, time enough to say a *Pater* and an *Ave,* or as long as a minute). Then all rise for the closing, which the deacon-narrator may sing solo to an elaborate melody.

Maundy Thursday

After sunset on Maundy Thursday, every parish church and the cathedral recall the Last Supper at a special eucharist. One or two deacons function as usual. On this day and all the sacred three days, two deacons attend the bishop who presides. A senior deacon proclaims the gospel, leads the intercessions, and ministers at the altar.

The ceremony of footwashing enacts the gospel of the *mandatum novum,* or new commandment, in John 13. In earlier centuries, those of high degree (kings, popes, bishops, abbots) washed the feet of those of low degree (peasants, seminarians, novices). More recently, the parish priest washed the feet of parishioners.

The ceremony varies according to the customs of the parish. Deacons organize, help at, and in some places perform the ceremony. They may change the introduction (BOS 91) to invite others to wash feet. In some places, a few members of the congregation are chosen to have their feet washed, usually by the presider. In other places, the people informally come and go to a large tub in full view, sit to have their feet washed, and kneel to wash the feet of others.

After the postcommunion prayer, the liturgy usually ends with reserving the sacrament for administration at the Good Friday liturgy. There are many ways of doing this. In one customary pattern, the presider puts on incense, kneels, and censes the sacrament. Kneeling, all sing "Now, my tongue, the mystery telling" (Hymn 329). Either during or after the hymn, a deacon (or the presider) rises and takes the sacrament from the altar. Accompanied by candles, the deacon carries it to a place apart from the main altar.

On Thursday and Friday during the sacred three days, the liturgy traditionally ends without a blessing (or prayer over the people) or dismissal. A deacon may help in stripping the altar, without ceremony. The liturgies of the Easter Triduum are acts in the paschal mystery of Christ. Intermissions of silence, fasting, and prayer separate the liturgies. The drama reaches a climax and ends at the Easter Vigil.

Good Friday

The presider and deacons (and two acolytes) enter silently, reverence the altar, and kneel before it, for at least a minute. Then they rise and go to their chairs. Readers proclaim the passion gospel as on Palm Sunday.

For the solemn intercessions, a deacon or deacons, standing at the usual place, sing or say the introduction and biddings. They may adapt the "For" clauses by changing some, adding some, and omitting some. After each bidding, a deacon may direct: "Let us kneel in silent prayer." After a significant period of silence (up to a minute), the same or another deacon commands: "Arise."

"If desired, a wooden cross may now be brought into the church and placed in the sight of the people" (BCP 281, BAS 313). The ceremony is known as veneration of the cross or meditation on the cross (BAS 313). It takes place simply or solemnly, in several ways. In one solemn form, a deacon goes to the entrance of the church and takes up a bare wooden cross. Flanked by two acolytes bearing candles, the deacon enters the church and walks slowly to the altar, pausing three times and lifting the cross. Each time, the deacon sings at a higher pitch: "Behold the wood of the cross, on which hung the savior of the world." The people respond: "Come, let us worship." (BAS 313 gives two texts.) After each response, everyone else kneels briefly in silence.

The deacon places the cross before the altar or in another convenient place in the sight of the people, between the candles. During the singing of anthems (see BAS 314–17), the people remain in their seats in meditation or come forward to kneel or bow before the cross and often to kiss or touch it.

"In the absence of a bishop or priest, all that precedes may be led by a deacon or lay reader" (BCP 282). In this liturgy, as in similar ones, a deacon presides only when the normal presider is absent.

If there is communion, after the singing of "Sing, my tongue, the glorious battle" (Hymn 165 or 166), a deacon rises and spreads the cloth on the bare altar. The deacon carries the reserved sacrament to the altar

and places it on the cloth, all in silence. Two acolytes
with candles accompany the deacon and place the candles on or near the altar. The presider comes to the
altar for the confession of sin and the Lord's Prayer.
After communion, deacons and others consume the remaining sacrament (unless there is to be another liturgy
that day), clear the altar, and cleanse the vessels. After
the final prayers, all go in silence, without dismissal.

Holy Saturday

The proper liturgy of the word appropriately takes
the place of the noonday office. After the entrance,
there may be a period of silence, and

> the silence may be bid in this manner. Facing the
> people, the celebrant chants, "Let us pray." The
> deacon (or celebrant) then sings "Let us kneel in
> silent prayer." At the conclusion of the silence the
> deacon chants "Arise." All then stand; and the cele-
> brant chants the Collect of the Day. [*Prayer Book
> Office* 109-110]

The deacon announces the gospel, "The Conclusion of
the Passion of our Lord Jesus Christ according to
Matthew (or John)." The people omit the usual responses.

The Great Vigil of Easter

The Easter Vigil consists of four liturgies: light,
word, baptism, and eucharist. Carrying the paschal
candle and singing the Exsultet is the prerogative of
deacons, who also help according to order in baptism
and the eucharist (BCP 284, BAS 321).

Normally, the liturgy of light begins in darkness outside the church. Fire is kindled, and the presider addresses the people and says a prayer. In some places,
the presider cuts a cross in the candle, traces the Greek
letters *alpha* and *omega* and the numbers of the year,

and inserts five grains of incense in the wax. (See rites in BAS 333.) The presider or a deacon lights the paschal candle from the new fire.

Carrying the candle, the deacon leads the people into church, pausing three times and singing, each time at a higher pitch: "The light of Christ." The people respond: "Thanks be to God." (Note the resemblance to the entrance of the cross on Good Friday.) The deacon pauses preferably at the start, the church door, and the chancel. At each pause, the deacon lifts the candle. (If the people gather indoors, the pauses take place at the entrance, halfway through the nave, and at the chancel.)

At the start, or before placing the candle in its stand near the lectern or pulpit, the deacon gives those nearby a chance to light their hand candles from the paschal candle. (In some places, the people light their candles before entering church, in others, they enter in near darkness.) The light spreads through the congregation, candle to candle.

The deacon puts the candle in its stand, goes to the presider (who has meanwhile come to the chair), and helps in putting incense on the coals. The deacon bows deeply before the presider to ask for a blessing. The presider replies: "The Lord be in your heart and on your lips that you may worthily proclaim his paschal praise: In the name of the Father, and of the Son, and of the Holy Spirit." Another blessing (as in the normal eucharist) goes: "May the Spirit of the Lord be upon you as you bring his paschal praise to the poor." The deacon replies: "Amen."

The deacon returns to the candle, takes the censer, and censes the candle by walking around it (if possible). Facing the people across the candle, the deacon sings the Exsultet. The deacon uses the altar book at the lectern or pulpit, or in the dimness sings from memory. In the introductory "Rejoice" stanzas, the deacon keeps hands joined; from the salutation onward, the deacon extends hands in the prayer gesture.

In some parishes, deacons change the text in two places: "fathers" becomes "ancestors," and "man is" becomes "human beings are." It is also common to add two traditional passages omitted in the prayer book version: (1) at the end of the first "How" stanza, "O happy fault, O necessary sin of Adam, which gained for us so great a redeemer," and (2) at the end of the phrase about the candle, "the work of the bees your creatures." (The Anglican Church of Canada allows deacons to use a different translation or musical setting, BAS 334.)

Deacons help at baptism (see chapter 2), and a deacon proclaims the gospel. After the epistle (and silence), a deacon may go to the presider and say: "[Sir or Madam or N.], I bring you a message of great joy, the message of alleluia." The presider or a cantor then sings alleluias, and the people repeat them.

The prayer book requires the prayers of the people in the Easter Vigil. Here and throughout the fifty days, the deacon sings or says the Easter dismissal with "alleluia, alleluia."

> In the absence of a bishop or priest, a deacon or lay reader may lead the first two parts of the service, the Renewal of Baptismal Vows, and the Ministry of the Word of the Vigil Eucharist, concluding with the Prayers of the People, the Lord's Prayer, and the Dismissal. A deacon may also, when the services of a priest cannot be obtained, and with the authorization of the bishop, officiate at public Baptism; and may administer Easter Communion from the Sacrament previously consecrated. (BCP 284, see BAS 321)

The Day of Pentecost: Whitsunday

If a vigil is held on Saturday night, deacons function as usual in the service of light, helping with incense. The paschal candle is already lit.

In many places, at some or all liturgies, several persons read the gospel in ancient and foreign languages. All gather at the ambo or other place of reading. A deacon announces the gospel in English (or other language of the congregation) and censes the book. Starting with the oldest language, the others then read, without announcement or closing. Finally, the deacon reads the gospel in the local language and gives the closing formula.

6

Deacons in Pastoral Liturgies

Reaffirmation of Baptismal Vows

The stages of reaffirmation are parallel to those of the catechumenate, described in chapter 2 (see BOS 132–41). The traditional role of deacons suggests that they function in two main ways: (1) They involve those preparing for reaffirmation in care of the poor, sick, and needy. (2) They include their names in the prayers of the people.

The liturgies of reaffirmation mention deacons only once. In the first stage, at the welcoming of baptized persons into the community, a deacon or sponsor calls out their names as they are written in the church register (BOS 137).

Confirmation

If enough deacons are available, two attend the bishop, and a senior deacon proclaims the gospel reading, leads the intercessions, and ministers at the altar (see chapter 3).

For the prayers of the candidates, a deacon may use the petitions from baptism. Because some of the petitions are redundant for those already baptized, it is better to omit them, as the prayer book allows (BCP 417, but BAS 627 requires a different litany). Galley, pp. 231–32, provides a form for the prayers of the people at baptism and confirmation.

A Form of Commitment to Christian Service

To the preceding prayers of the people, a deacon may add the name of the person making or renewing a commitment.

The Celebration and Blessing of a Marriage

In addition to reading the gospel and otherwise helping at the eucharist (if celebrated), a deacon may deliver the charge and ask for the declaration of consent (both at BCP 424). (The Canadian church reserves them to the presider, BAS 529.) A deacon "or other person appointed" reads the nuptial prayers of the people (BCP 429–30, BAS 533).

"When it is permitted by civil law that deacons may perform marriages, and no priest or bishop is available, a deacon may use the service which follows [the marriage rite], omitting the nuptial blessing which follows the Lord's Prayer" (BCP 422, see BAS 527). A similar rubric applies to the order for marriage (BCP 435). A deacon presides at a marriage only with the specific authorization of the bishop.

The Blessing of a Civil Marriage

The blessing takes place within the eucharist. For the prayers of the people, a deacon uses the nuptial prayers (BCP 434, see 428).

An Order for Marriage

A deacon helps as in normal marriage and may preside only under certain restrictions (see above). The order permits the composition of intercessions for the husband and wife, their life together, the church, and the world.

A Thanksgiving for the Birth or Adoption of a Child

In the eucharist, the liturgy follows the prayers of the people. A deacon may mention the names of the child and parents. (See also BOS 156.)

The Reconciliation of a Penitent

Each of the two forms for sacramental confession provides a "Declaration of Forgiveness to be used by a Deacon or Lay Person." The declaration is simply a statement to the penitent, after the confession, that Christ "forgives your sins" (BCP 448, 452, BAS 169, 171). A deacon uses the provision mainly in an emergency such as imminent death or isolated imprisonment, when a bishop or presbyter is unobtainable. Nevertheless, when pastoral prudence and charity lead a deacon to hear a confession, the deacon should first say clearly that the confessor will declare forgiveness but not pronounce absolution. "The secrecy of a confession is morally absolute for the confessor, and must under no circumstances be broken" (BCP 446, BAS 166).

If, for sound reason, sacramental confession, or at least absolution, takes place in the presence of a congregation, a deacon functions as usual in the preceding liturgy of the word and the following liturgy of the sacrament. The true goal, and climax, of reconciliation is rejoining in communion.

Ministration to the Sick

Bishops and presbyters provide the main sacramental and pastoral care of the sick. From early times, however, deacons and other baptized persons have visited and cared for the sick. Ideally, the church in all her orders and ministries comes to the bedside for prayer, anointing, and communion. As a practical reality, the visitor, whether bishop, presbyter, deacon, or any baptized person, functions visibly as a sign of the church beyond the sickroom. Often today, deacons visit the sick in close cooperation with presbyters and other persons. They also organize, train, and lead teams of baptized ministers. In such an arrangement, a deacon may function as liturgist, whose pastoral visit culminates in a rite of word and sacrament.

Ministration to the sick consists of three liturgies— word, laying on of hands and anointing, and communion—used separately or (preferably) together. A deacon chooses among four sets of readings—each with epistle, psalm, and gospel—or any other passage of scripture. The deacon needs to use only part of a set. A few verses (such as the angel passage in Psalm 91) provide material for comment on the Christian meaning of sickness and death. The deacon may then offer prayers (several are given in BCP 458–60) or a litany, mentioning the sick person. The deacon may help the sick person make a general confession. (For the restricted use of sacramental confession, see above.)

Bishops and parish presbyters (the elders of James 5:14) lay hands on and anoint the sick. Ancient custom, common sense, and the prayer book also give the ministry to deacons and other baptized persons. "In cases of necessity, a deacon or lay person may perform the anointing, using oil blessed by a bishop or priest" (BCP 456, see BAS 555). Since necessity occurs whenever a person is seriously ill or preparing for surgery, deacons should seize the opportunity to offer this sign of Christian health.

Oil of the sick, soaked in a wad of cotton, is usually carried in a small vessel of precious metal. A deacon dips a thumb in the oil and marks a cross on the sick person's forehead, saying the anointing sentence. It is sometimes necessary to anoint another place on the body, the back of the hand or the site of the sickness.

The deacon may point out that the sign of the cross on the forehead recalls the signing in baptism, and that we receive true healing through union with Christ and his church. In ancient times, Christians used copious amounts of pure olive oil, and sick persons sometimes drank it like medicine.

(Although the prayer book appears to reserve the laying on of hands to priests, it allows deacons and others to use anointing. The term "anointing" stands for the entire rite, as does "unction" in the catechism, BCP 861. In a public service, baptized persons with a gift of healing may join in laying on hands, BOS 151. BAS 555 allows anyone to use the entire rite. Deacons thus should also lay on hands.)

After the anointing, the deacon opens the pyx and begins the communion rite with the Lord's Prayer, first saying: "Let us pray in the words our Savior Christ has taught us." The deacon gives communion with the usual words. If the person is near death, the deacon may use "other words" (see BCP 399). From ancient times, Christians have referred to the final communion of a dying person as *viaticum* (provisions for a journey). The deacon gives communion with these or similar words: "N., receive this food for your journey, the body of Christ, the bread of heaven." For the wine, the deacon adds: "The blood of Christ, the cup of salvation."

If the sick person is unable to receive the sacrament, the deacon "is to assure that person that all the benefits of Communion are received, even though the Sacrament is not received with the mouth" (BCP 457). Others in the sickroom may also receive. Communion ends with a prayer and "Let us bless the Lord."

Unless coming straight from a nearby eucharist, a deacon ordinarily wears street clothes. If a stole is worn, a deacon wears it in the manner of a deacon.

Ministration at the Time of Death

If the person is near death, a deacon should give communion immediately, followed by the several prayers. If there is time, a deacon may use the prayers with the three parts of the ministration to the sick: (1) at the end of the word, the prayer for a person near death and the litany at the time of death; (2) just before communion, the Lord's Prayer and collect "Deliver your servant"; (3) in place of the postcommunion prayer and dismissal, the three commendatory prayers.

The Burial of the Dead

Burial of the dead is a series of liturgies or stations along the journey. If possible, the vigil (or wake) takes place at the home of the dead person, or in church on the night before burial. A deacon uses the litany at the time of death or the litany provided for a vigil (BCP 465); the people may need a copy of these prayers. Either litany may take place within evening prayer, said or sung or celebrated solemnly. If incense is used at the candle-lighting, a deacon also censes the body by walking around it.

Reception of the body takes place on the arrival of the body at church. A deacon or other person (such as a family member) leads the procession bearing the lighted paschal candle. When the body reaches a resting place before the altar, the deacon places the candle in its stand nearby. A deacon also places the book of gospels open on the coffin.

In the burial eucharist, deacons function as usual. A deacon proclaims the gospel reading from the book open on the coffin. A deacon or other person sings or says the prayers of the people, using one of three forms (BCP 465, 480, 497, see BAS 579, 593). The Rite Two form is suitable if the gospel reading has been John 11:21–27 ("I am the resurrection and the life"). If incense is used at the offertory, the deacon (or presider) may conclude by walking around the body.

The eucharist ends with the commendation, at which the presider, deacons, and other ministers come to stand near the body. During the singing of the *kontakion* "Give rest, O Christ," if the presider sprinkles the body with water or censes it, a deacon helps in the usual way. A deacon dismisses the people with "Let us go forth in the name of Christ."

"When the services of a priest cannot be obtained, a deacon or lay reader may preside at the service" (BCP 455, 468, see BAS 571).

In the committal, deacons may take parts not assigned to the presider. A deacon may locate some real dirt and distribute it for casting on the coffin.

The Burial of a Deacon

The body of a deacon is dressed in Easter vestments, placed in a simple coffin, and as soon as possible brought to the cathedral or parish church. The bishop, with deacons, receives the body at the church door and escorts it to a place before the altar. Deacons may carry the coffin.

At the vigil, the bishop, attended by two deacons, and with other deacons as choir, celebrates solemn evensong. Traditional propers for evensong of the dead are given in *The Prayer Book Office,* p. 348. In the absence of the bishop, a presbyter or senior deacon officiates at the reception and vigil. Deacons and others close to the life and ministry of the dead deacon help.

At the burial eucharist, two deacons attend the presider (preferably the bishop). When a bishop presides, a senior deacon serves as usual (see chapter 3). Other deacons gather in the chancel or nearby and form a choir for the liturgy. Presbyters of the diocese may concelebrate. Family members (bake the bread and) present the bread and wine. Incense is appropriate.

At the commendation, the presider and all the deacons gather near the body. Deacons carry the coffin out of church or escort the body and, if possible, complete the burial by taking part in the committal at the grave.

An Order for Burial

If the rite includes the eucharist, deacons help as in normal burial.

Other Pastoral Liturgies

Welcoming New People to a Congregation (BOS 110). A deacon may mention their names in the prayers of the people.

When Members Leave a Congregation (BOS 111). On their last Sunday, a deacon may mention their departure before the prayers of the people and add their names to the petitions.

Celebration for a Home (BOS 142–52). The prayers during the procession through the house take the place of the prayers of the people. The blessing of the house appropriately takes place within the eucharist, in which a deacon functions as usual. (BOS also provides home blessings for Epiphany and Easter, without the eucharist, 45–48, 97–100.)

Blessing of Parents at the Beginning of Pregnancy (BOS 153–54, 155–56). The blessing takes place within the eucharist. A deacon may mention the father and mother in the prayers of the people.

Anniversary of a Marriage (BOS 159–61). The liturgy takes place within the eucharist. At a principal service, a deacon may add the names of the husband and wife to the prayers of the people.

A Public Service of Healing (BOS 162–69). If the service takes place within the eucharist, deacons function as usual. A litany of healing, led by a person appointed, may replace the prayers of the people.

Burial of One Who Does Not Profess the Christian Faith (BOS 171–74). A deacon functions mainly by proclaiming the only gospel reading provided, John 10:11–16.

Commissioning for Lay Ministries in the Church (BOS 175–91). A deacon who has a pastoral connection with the ministers, such as leading or training them in ministry, may act as sponsor in presenting them for commissioning. A deacon may mention them in the prayers of the people.

Dedication of Church Furnishings and Ornaments (BOS 192–209). Deacons accompany and help the presider, especially when the bishop dedicates an altar or font. At the end of the dedication, "the benefactors and persons to be commemorated may be remembered in the Prayers of the People" (BOS 208).

The Founding of a Church (BOS 210–16). During the procession to the site where ground is to be broken, a deacon or other person sings or says the litany for the church. A deacon dismisses the people.

Restoring of Things Profaned (BOS 217–18). Deacons help with water or incense, used as signs of purification.

Securalizing a Consecrated Building (BOS 219–20). If the bishop presides, deacons help as usual.

7

Deacons in Episcopal Liturgies

All liturgies are episcopal, since a bishop presides whenever possible. Even when the bishop is absent, the assembly gathers around the leadership of the bishop, delegated to a presbyter.

Some liturgies require the presidency of a bishop. The ordination rites present the church with an opportunity to display the three orders as distinct ministries with special responsibilities and special significance. The three orders are "a gift from God for the nurture of his people and the proclamation of the Gospel everywhere" (BCP 510, BAS 631). To paraphrase Ignatius of Antioch and Cyprian of Carthage, where the catholic church is, there are bishops and presbyters and deacons and all the assembly of God's people.

The Ordination of a Bishop

"Representatives of the presbyterate, diaconate, and laity of the diocese for which the new bishop is to be consecrated, are assigned appropriate duties in the service" (BCP 511, BAS 632). A deacon or a priest (not a bishop) proclaims the gospel. At the offertory, deacons prepare the table and gifts, and a deacon dismisses the people.

Although it is possible to ordain a bishop with only one deacon, several are desirable. As many as five may serve as major assistants. Two attend the chief consecrator throughout the rite. After the prayer of consecration, two other deacons attend the new bishop, helping in the vesting and giving of symbols. (Where it is the custom, the same two deacons may hold the book of gospels open and face down over the head of the bishop-elect during the hymn *Veni Creator Spiritus.* Although in the Roman rite this ceremony takes place during the prayer of consecration, in Anglican usage it interferes with the laying on of hands at that point.) Another deacon helps as usual by proclaiming the gospel and ministering at the altar (see chapter 3). Other deacons, if present, give communion.

The Ordination of a Priest

A deacon or a priest (if deacons are absent) proclaims the gospel and dismisses the people, and deacons prepare the table. Two deacons attend the ordaining bishop. A senior deacon helps as usual by proclaiming the gospel and ministering at the altar (see chapter 3). Other deacons, if present, give communion.

The new priest joins the bishop at the altar for the eucharistic prayer and fraction. When a deacon ministers on the right, the priest stands on the left side of the bishop.

The Ordination of a Deacon

Deacons chosen for the diaconate normally are ordained separately from deacons chosen for the priesthood. In some dioceses, however, the bishop uses a single liturgy to ordain deacons and priests and commission other ministers in a parish, emphasizing their equality in a team.

The presence of other deacons supports the deacon-elect joining their company. Two deacons attend the bishop, and a senior deacon proclaims the gospel reading. Other deacons walk in procession ahead of the bishop, stand near the bishop in the chancel, and give communion. Although deacons do not join in laying on hands, their company symbolizes a family relationship among themselves and with their bishop. The active participation of the deacon-elect's spouse and children, if any, and others who serve in Christ emphasizes *diakonia* as a function of the Christian community.

The ordination takes place either in the cathedral or in the deacon-elect's parish on a Sunday, feast day, or other day when many persons can attend. The deacon-elect wears a surplice or preferably alb. Dalmatic and stole are laid out near the altar.

The deacon-elect walks ahead of the deacon carrying the book of gospels. A priest and an unordained person "and additional presenters if desired" (BCP 538, BAS 653), who may include deacons, present the deacon-elect to the bishop. A deacon or other person sings the litany for ordinations "or some other approved litany" (BCP 539). (The Canadian church provides a choice of two litanies, to be sung after the examination, BAS 656.) During the litany, the deacon-elect kneels (with everyone else) or sometimes lies prostrate. (According to ancient custom, all others remain standing during the fifty days of Easter and on Sundays.) Drawing from the scripture readings, the bishop normally preaches on the meaning and duties of the diaconate; someone else, including a deacon, may preach instead.

At the examination the deacon-elect, unattended and preferably without a book or program, stands before the bishop. An assisting deacon should hold the book, unless the deacon-elect memorizes the responses.

Then the deacon-elect kneels before the bishop. The people sing one of two hymns (usually *Veni Creator Spiritus*). A period of silent prayer follows. The bishop sings or says the prayer of consecration. At the epiclesis, the bishop lays hands on the head of the deacon-elect: "Therefore, Father, through Jesus Christ your Son, give your Holy Spirit to N.; fill *him* with

grace and power, and make *him* a deacon in your
Church" (BCP 545, see BAS 657).

After the consecration, other deacons, the spouse,
or others vest the new deacon in stole and dalmatic.
The bishop presents a Bible. (Historically, the bishop
presented the book of gospels from the altar). In some
places the bishop presents a towel and basin and uses
them to wash the feet of the new deacons, as they sit
in turn in the bishop's chair.

At the peace, the new deacon may exchange an
embrace first with the bishop, then with presbyters and
other deacons, then with spouse and others. As the
first liturgical act, the new deacon may direct all present to exchange the kiss of peace.

From then on, the new deacon prepares the table,
serves at the bishop's right side, consumes the remaining elements and cleanses the vessels, sings or says the
dismissal, accompanies the bishop out of church, and
may carry the sacrament to those who were absent. As
supervisor of lay eucharistic ministers, the deacon may
give them the sacrament to carry to the absent. If eucharistic prayer D is used (Canadian prayer 6), the
bishop names the new deacon in the remembrance
clauses.

If the bishop ordains two or more deacons, they
double up and share functions. Each deacon-elect has a
set of presenters. The bishop lays on hands and says
the epiclesis over each deacon-elect and then continues
with the rest of the prayer. All the new deacons stand
behind or near the altar. Depending on the number ordained, two deacons replace the two attending the
bishop, and at least one prepares the table and gifts. "If
there are many deacons, some assist in the Offertory
and others administer Holy Communion. One, appointed by the bishop, is to say the dismissal" (BCP
554, see BAS 666).

Celebration of a New Ministry

The rite is used mainly to institute presbyters as rectors of parishes. On occasion, it may also be used to install a deacon into a parish, chaplaincy, or other ministry. "The new minister, if a deacon, should read the Gospel, prepare the elements at the Offertory, assist the celebrant at the Altar, and dismiss the congregation" (BCP 558). The assembly gives symbols appropriate for the diaconate, such as a book of gospels, a towel and basin, an oil stock. Elsewhere, "deacons assist according to their order" (BCP 558).

The Dedication and Consecration of a Church

Deacons attend the bishop as usual and function according to order. For the prayers of the people, "some other form may be composed for the occasion, having due regard for the distinctive nature of the community, and with commemoration of benefactors, donors, artists, artisans, and others" (BCP 576).

Other Episcopal Liturgies

Consecration of Chrism Apart from Baptism (BOS 224–26, BAS 616-22). The rite takes place after the postcommunion prayer in the eucharist. "If desired, the vessel of oil may be brought forward in the offertory procession, received by a deacon or other minister, and then placed on a convenient side table until needed" (BOS 209). After the postcommunion prayer, a deacon brings the vessel to the bishop and, according to an old custom, may say aloud: "The oil for the holy chrism." (In Canada, the blessing of oils occurs near the end of the eucharistic prayer.)

In some places, the rite takes place at a chrism mass, on Maundy Thursday or earlier in Holy Week. The bishop blesses chrism for the whole diocese during the coming year, or for baptisms throughout the diocese at the Easter Vigil. If the bishop also blesses oil of the sick, the deacon brings the vessel to the bishop and may say aloud: "The oil of the sick."

Reaffirmation of Ordination Vows (BOS 227–30). The rite is used at a gathering of presbyters (and deacons) with their bishop. It is appropriate in the eucharist at a conference or retreat or at the college of presbyters. Sometimes it takes place at the chrism mass on Maundy Thursday or earlier in Holy Week. In some dioceses, the bishop and deacons reaffirm their vows at a separate meeting of the community of deacons. The practice avoids confusing deacons with presbyters.

Two deacons attend the bishop, and a senior deacon helps as usual by proclaiming the gospel and ministering at the altar (see chapter 3). The intercessions may be omitted.

The bishop may also use the rite to receive a priest (but not a deacon) from another communion, or to restore a presbyter or deacon to the ministry. The bishop greets a newly restored deacon at the peace. The deacon, "properly vested, prepares the bread and wine at the Offertory" (BOS 230).

A Service for the Ending of a Pastoral Relationship and Leave-taking from a Congregation (BOS 233–40). Two deacons normally attend the bishop, if present, and a senior deacon functions as usual in the eucharist. If the bishop is absent, a deacon may act as the bishop's deputy.

Recognition and Investiture of a Diocesan Bishop (BOS 242–49). In its fullest use, the rite provides for the recognition, investiture, and seating (in the cathedral) of a bishop. "Representative presbyters, deacons, and lay persons are assigned appropriate duties in the service" (BOS 242). From the start, the knocking on the door, the new bishop is "attended by two deacons" (BOS 243). Deacons prepare the table and gifts, and a deacon dismisses the people.

Welcoming and Seating of a Bishop in the Cathedral (BOS 250–53). Used separately, the rite completes the recognition and investiture of a diocesan bishop. Again the new bishop, from the knocking on the door, is "attended by two deacons" (BOS 251). A deacon dismisses the people.

Setting Apart for a Special Vocation (BOS 254–58). Two deacons normally attend the bishop. If the rite occurs within the eucharist, a senior deacon functions as usual.